Contents

North America is a continent   4

Early North America   6

North America today   8

The land   10

The climate   12

Plants and animals   14

The people   16

The countries   18

Regions

The North   20

Mexico and the Caribbean   24

Central America   26

North America's future   28

North America in review   30

Websites   30

Glossary   31

Index   32

Glossary words

When a word is printed in **bold**, you can look up its meaning in the Glossary on page 31.

North America is a continent

North America is the third largest continent in the world. Look at a world map or globe and you can see the world is made up of water and land. The big areas of land are called continents. There are seven continents:

- ⊕ Africa
- ⊕ Antarctica
- ⊕ Asia
- ⊕ Australia
- ⊕ Europe
- ⊕ North America
- ⊕ South America.

Borders

The borders of continents follow natural physical features such as coastlines and mountain ranges. Most of North America's borders are oceans:

- ⊕ Arctic Ocean
- ⊕ Atlantic Ocean
- ⊕ Pacific Ocean.

North America has one land border where Panama joins Colombia in South America.

World map showing the seven modern-day continents

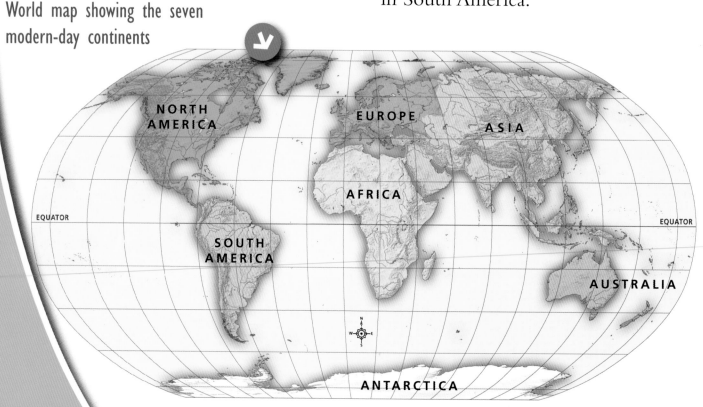

The world is a jigsaw

The Earth's crust is made up of huge plates, called **tectonic plates**, which fit together like a jigsaw puzzle. These plates are constantly moving, up and down and sideways, up to 10 centimetres (4 inches) a year. Over long periods of time, the plates change in size and shape as their edges push against each other.

Around 250 million years ago, there was one massive supercontinent called Pangaea. Around 200 million years ago it began splitting and formed two continents. Laurasia was the northern continent and Gondwana was the southern continent. By about 65 million years ago, Laurasia and Gondwana had separated into smaller landmasses that look much like the continents we know today. Laurasia split to form Europe, Asia and North America. Gondwana split to form South America, Africa, Australia and Antarctica.

North America was once part of the supercontinent Pangaea.

The North American continent formed when Laurasia split into smaller landmasses.

Early North America

When the continents were one, animals moved across the land, as there was no water to stop them. When the continents split apart, the animals were left on separate landmasses and they began to change and develop into the animals we know today. During this time dinosaurs roamed the Earth including North America. As dinosaurs became **extinct** other animals took over. An ancestor of the horse called merychippus grazed on grass in North America. It had three toes on each foot. Later, horse-like animals called a pliohippus developed hoofs, which made it easier for them to run fast over the flat land.

What's in a word?

America was named after an Italian man, Amerigo Vespucci. He sailed to America around the same time as Christopher Columbus.

Early humans

Scientists believe modern humans, or *Homo sapiens*, came from Africa. Scientists think that humans spread from Africa through Asia to North America around 15 000 years ago. These people hunted animals, caught fish and gathered plants for food.

The merychippus, or three-toed horse, lived around 200 million years ago.

6

Monte Alban was a Zapotec city.

The Maya lived in the large city of Tikal around 2000 years ago.

First civilisations

Around 6500 years ago, early humans in North America discovered how to grow crops such as wheat and corn. Groups of people moved together to help each other grow crops and for protection. Eventually, small settlements grew into towns and cities. These became the start of early civilisations. The first North American civilisations were in the southern regions in countries such as Mexico and Guatemala.

Early North American civilisations

These ancient civilisations lived in Mexico and Central America from 3400 to 500 years ago. The civilisations overlapped each other but existed in this order:

⊕ Olmecs built stone buildings and carved large stone heads to represent Gods

⊕ Mixtecs and Zapotecs carved patterns in the walls of buildings

⊕ the **Maya** built many stone cities such as Tikal in Guatemala and Palenque in Mexico. They farmed land and invented a calendar

⊕ Aztecs worshipped the sun and moon.

North America today

Second biggest country

Canada is the second biggest country in the world. Northern parts are very cold so most Canadian people live in the south, near the border of the United States of America.

North America is the third biggest continent in the world. It is 25 million square kilometres (9.3 million square miles) in size. There are 23 countries in the region known as North America. This includes Central America, which joins the North with South America, and the many islands in the Caribbean Sea. The largest country is Canada at 9 976 140 square kilometres (3 852 788 square miles). The smallest country is Grenada, a tiny island of only 340 square kilometres (131 square miles).

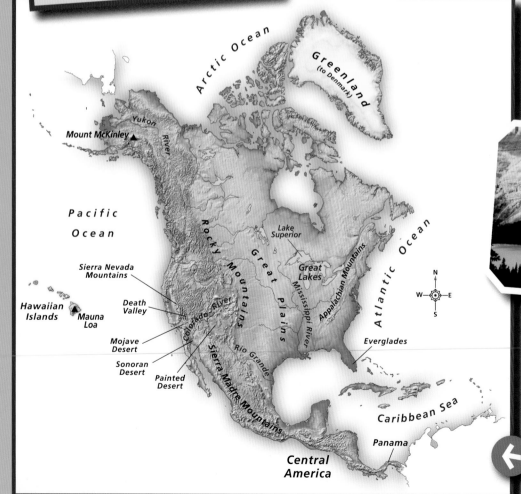

Arctic Ocean

Greenland (to Denmark)

Yukon River

Mount McKinley

Pacific Ocean

Lake Superior

Sierra Nevada Mountains

Rocky Mountains

Great Plains

Great Lakes

Appalachian Mountains

Atlantic Ocean

Hawaiian Islands
Mauna Loa

Death Valley

Colorado River

Mojave Desert

Sonoran Desert

Painted Desert

Sierra Madre Mountains

Rio Grande

Mississippi River

Everglades

N
W — E
S

Caribbean Sea

Panama

Central America

Peyto Lake in Canada is this colour because of glacial silt deposits.

The physical features of the North American continent

8

Tehipite Dome (left) is made of granite.

Physical features

North America is in the **Northern Hemisphere**. The northern part of North America lies inside the Arctic Circle, which is a land of ice and snow called the **tundra**. Big mountain ranges run down the western side of North America through Alaska, Canada and the United States of America. Mountains also run down the eastern side of North America. In between these mountains are plains or flat land. In the south-west of North America there are dry deserts. North America has many rivers, lakes and swamps scattered around the continent.

Americans enjoy spending sunny days at Santa Monica Pier in California.

North American people

More than 480 million people live in North America. The first Americans were **Native Americans**. They were joined by the Spanish and other Europeans, who brought with them African people to work as **slaves** on farms. Later, **migrants** also came to North America. Today, North America has a mix of many different **ethnic groups**.

The land

The North American continent covers a huge area and has many different types of landforms.

Mountains

Mountain ranges stretch along the western side of North America, including the:

⊕ Rocky Mountains
⊕ Sierra Madre Mountains
⊕ Sierra Nevada Mountains.

On the eastern side of the United States of America are the smaller Appalachian Mountains. The Hawaiian Islands also have volcanoes. Mount Mauna Loa in Hawaii erupts about every four years.

This lake is situated high in the Sierra Nevada Mountains.

The highest mountain

The highest mountain in North America is Mount McKinley in Alaska, United States of America. It is 6194 metres (20 322 feet) high.

Deserts

Lying east of the Sierra Nevada Mountains in California are hot and dry deserts. These deserts include:

⊕ Mojave Desert
⊕ Painted Desert
⊕ Sonora Desert.

Plains

Down the middle of North America is a series of flat plains that are used for farming. This region is called the Great Plains.

Rivers

The longest river in North America is the Mississippi River at 6019 kilometres (3740 miles). It is the fourth longest river in the world. Other big rivers flowing through Canada, the United States of America and Mexico are the:

🌐 Colorado River
🌐 Rio Grande
🌐 Yukon River.

Lakes

North America has many lakes, particularly in Canada. The biggest group of lakes is on the Canadian border. Together these lakes are called the Great Lakes and include:

🌐 Lake Eerie
🌐 Lake Huron
🌐 Lake Michigan
🌐 Lake Ontario
🌐 Lake Superior (biggest lake in North America).

Lake Atitlan in Guatemala was once a volcano.

Other lakes are scattered around the continent. Some lakes in Central America were formed when water from rain filled old volcano craters. Lake Atitlan in Guatemala and Crater Lake in the United States of America were both formed that way.

Swamps

The Everglades is a swampy area in the south of the United States of America. There are also swamps in the Darien region of Panama.

The climate

North America's huge area means there are many different climates. They range from ice and snow in the north to hot and wet in the south.

Arctic

Most of Canada and Alaska (in the United States of America) have a cold **arctic** climate. The north is covered in snow and ice, except for a short time in summer.

⬆

Winter snowfall in a forest of the Sierra Nevada Mountains.

Tornado Alley

Tornadoes are twisting funnels of wind that come from big thunderstorms. They bring winds that destroy buildings and kill people. Most tornadoes happen in early summer in the middle part of the United States of America. They are so common here that this region is called Tornado Alley.

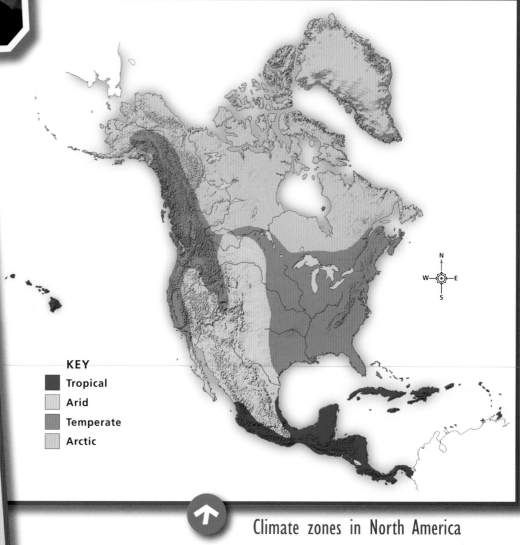

KEY
- ⬛ Tropical
- ⬜ Arid
- ⬛ Temperate
- ⬜ Arctic

⬆

Climate zones in North America

Temperate

The eastern side of North America south of Canada has a **temperate** climate with warm, **humid** summers. Winters are cold, especially in the north. Cities such as New York sometimes get snow blizzards.

Arid

The deserts of North America have an **arid** climate. Summers are very hot and dry. Temperatures up to 43°C (110°F) are common. Rain may not fall for many years. In winter, deserts in North America can get very cold, especially at night.

Tropical

Central America, the state of Florida and parts of Mexico have a **tropical** climate. These areas are hot and humid with rain all year round.

Some plants are able to survive in the desert conditions of New Mexico, United States of America.

Hot and cold temperature facts

The second hottest temperature ever recorded in the world was in 1913 in the desert of Death Valley, United States of America. It reached 57°C (134°F).

The coldest temperature recorded in North America was at a place called Snag in Canada. The temperature in February 1947 dropped to –62°C (–81°F).

13

Plants and animals

The tallest redwood

The redwood pine tree grows near the west coast of North America and is the world's tallest tree. One tree in California is 112 metres (367 feet) tall.

North America is a land of many different plants and animals.

Arctic tundra

The cold windy weather stops trees growing tall so plants in the Arctic are small.

Some animals grow white fur or feathers to help them hide in the snowy environment. Arctic animals include the arctic fox, polar bear and snowy owl.

Forests

Different types of trees grow in forest areas. **Coniferous** trees such as pine and fir grow in colder areas. **Deciduous** trees such as maple and aspen prefer warmer weather.

Bears live in some North American forests. The Kodiak bear reaches 3 metres (9 feet) tall when standing upright. Smaller animals such as raccoons eat fruit, lizards and birds.

Redwood trees are coniferous trees living near the west coast of the United States of America.

Raccoons are common in North America.

Tropical rainforest

Tropical rainforests grow in a tropical climate. Tall trees grow close together and block out the sun below. Shade loving plants such as palms and ferns grow under the trees.

A rich variety of animals live in the trees and on the forest floor. The jaguar is a large spotted cat that hunts smaller animals such as deer and wild pigs called peccaries. Monkeys and parrots live in the treetops.

Jaguars live in the rainforests of Central America.

Desert

Plants and animals of the deserts have learned to live with hot temperatures and little rain. The giant saguaro cactus plant stores water in its spiky stems.

Animals such as jumping mice avoid the heat by staying underground during the day and coming out at night to find seeds to eat. Poisonous rattlesnakes catch mice to eat. The roadrunner bird has long strong legs that allow it to run very fast. It eats lizards and sometimes snakes.

A grasshopper on a cactus in Mexico. The green part of the cactus plant stores water.

The people

North America is a continent of many people with many different beliefs, **traditions** and languages.

Ethnic groups

Native Americans were the original people of North America. They moved around the continent and separated into different tribes such as:

- Apache
- Inuits or Eskimos
- Lacandon Indians
- Navaho.

From the 1700s, people from European countries such as England, France and Spain **colonised** North America. The Africans were officially slaves there until 1863. **Ancestors** of these slaves are called African–Americans. Since 1900, millions of people have migrated to North America from Europe and Asia.

People facts	
Population	481 million people
Most populated country	United States of America with 286 million people
Least populated country	Saint Kitts and Nevis with 44 000 people
Most crowded country	Island of Barbados in the Caribbean with 628 people per square kilometre (1626 people per square mile)

Lacandon Indians originated in South East Mexico.

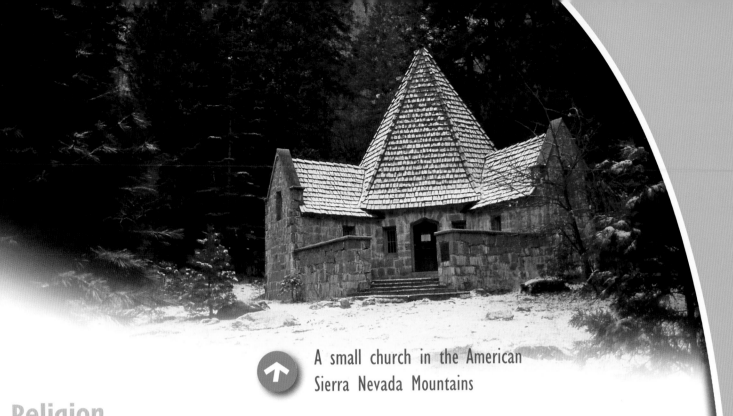

A small church in the American Sierra Nevada Mountains

Religion

Europeans brought Christianity to North America. Most people follow some form of the Christian religion. Christians believe in the teachings of Jesus as the Son of God.

Many Native Americans still follow some traditional beliefs. The Navaho and the Maya believe in nature gods. These people see gods in landmarks such as mountains and rivers. They also worship their dead ancestors.

Languages

The two main languages spoken in North America came from Europe. Spanish is spoken throughout Mexico, Central America and some of the Caribbean Islands. English is the official language of the United States of America and Canada. The Canadians of Quebec speak French. There are also many local languages such as Navaho and Inuit. Guatemalan Indians speak Mayan.

The inside of this Catholic church in Oaxaca, Mexico, is covered in **gold leaf** and paint.

17

The countries

There are 23 North American countries. Ten are on the mainland of the continent and there are 13 **independent** island countries in the Caribbean Sea. North America is divided into the following regions:

⊕ the North   ⊕ Mexico and the Caribbean   ⊕ Central America.

Independence

After North America and South America were discovered, the European countries Spain, England and France ruled the region. The stronger, better-armed Europeans destroyed the original civilisations, such as the Aztecs. The United States of America was the first of these countries to become independent after the American War of Independence against England in 1776. In the 1830s, Spain was forced to let Mexico and the Central American countries have their independence as well. The French gave Canada to the English in 1763. Canada became independent from England in 1867 but continues to belong to the **Commonwealth**. Some countries have only recently become independent, such as Grenada in 1974 and Belize in 1981.

KEY
- United States of America
- Canada
- Mexico and the Caribbean
- Central America

CANADA

UNITED STATES OF AMERICA

MEXICO

BAHAMAS
CUBA
JAMAICA
BELIZE
HONDURAS
NICARAGUA
GUATEMALA
EL SALVADOR
COSTA RICA
PANAMA
HAITI
DOMINICAN REPUBLIC
ST KITTS and NEVIS
ANTIGUA and BARBUDA
DOMINICA
BARBADOS
GRENADA
ST VINCENT and THE GRENADINES

North American regions and countries

 These are Native American buildings called Casa Grande in Arizona. They belong to the Hohokam people.

Land ownership

When the Europeans first came to North America many took the land from the native people by force. Recently, many people from **indigenous groups** have fought to have their land returned. In Canada, the state of Nunavut has been handed back to the Inuit people. In the United States of America, some Native Americans live on special areas of land called reserves.

Fighting for land

Fighting in some North American countries has caused many deaths and much hardship for the people. The fighting is caused by arguments over land ownership. In Chiapas, a region in South East Mexico, some ethnic groups have been fighting the **government** to have their land returned to them. Other countries were run by cruel leaders who treated people badly. People fought to replace these leaders, in Nicaragua, El Salvador and Guatemala during the 1980s.

The North

There are 2 countries in the North of North America. Use the key below to find out about and compare each country's languages, religions, ethnic groups, agriculture and natural resources.

Country	Languages	Religions	Ethnic groups	Agriculture	Natural resources
Canada	■ ■ ■	✝ ☼ ☾	🧍 🧍 🧍	✣ ♣ ✪ ☆	◆◇◆◇◆◆◇ ◆◆💧◇◆◇
United States of America	■ ■ ■	✝ ✡ ☾	🧍 🧍 🧍 🧍 🧍	✣ ♣ ✳ ☆ ✪ ◎ ✪	◆◇◆◇◆◇ ◆◆💧◇◆◇

Key	Languages	Religions	Ethnic groups	Agriculture	Natural resources
	■ English	✝ Christian	🧍 African–American	✣ Cereal grains	◇ Bauxite or Alumina
	■ French	✡ Jewish	🧍 Native American	✪ Citrus	◆ Coal
	■ Spanish	☾ Islam	🧍 Asian	✳ Coffee	◇ Copper
	■ Traditional languages	☼ Traditional beliefs	🧍 English	◎ Cotton	◇ Diamonds
			🧍 French	✪ Dairy	◇ Gold
			🧍 Hispanic	♣ Fruit and vegetables	◆ **Hydropower**
				☆ Sheep, cattle and goats	◆ Iron ore
					◆ Lead
					◇ Nickel
					💧 Oil and gas
					◆ Phosphates
					◇ Silver
					◇ Timber
					◆ Uranium
					◆ Zinc

Canada in focus

Official name: Canada

Area: 9 976 140 square kilometres (3 851 788 square miles)

Population: 32 million people

Capital: Ottawa

Major cities: Vancouver, Montreal, Quebec, Toronto, Edmonton

Colonial rule: England, France

Famous landmarks: Rocky Mountains, Great Lakes, Niagara Falls

Famous people: Jim Carrey, Keanu Reeves, Michael J. Fox (actors), Shania Twain (musician)

Traditions: ice fishing, kayaking, ice hockey

Traditional food: Quebec is the world's largest producer of maple syrup

Most of Canada is made up of flat plains around Hudson Bay. The Rocky Mountains are on the western side of the country. Most people in Canada live in cities.

High-rise apartments provide housing for many people in Vancouver, Canada.

Kayaking is a popular pastime in British Columbia, Canada.

The United States of America covers an area of 9 629 047 square kilometres (3 717 796 square miles) and is the third largest country in the world. It consists of 50 states that vary widely in size and population. The United States of America stretches across central North America from the Atlantic Ocean in the east to the Pacific Ocean in the West, and from Canada in the north to Mexico and the Gulf of Mexico in the south. The state of Alaska is located in the north-west of North America.

The United States of America in focus

Official name: United States of America

Area: 9 372 610 square kilometres
(3 618 765 square miles)

Population: 292 million

Capital: Washington DC

Major cities: New York, Los Angeles,
Chicago, Dallas, Seattle, Miami

Colonial rule: Spain, England

Famous landmarks: The White House in
Washington DC, Golden Gate Bridge in
San Francisco, Empire State Building in
New York, Grand Canyon in Arizona

Famous people: Tiger Woods (golfer),
Michael Jordan (basketball player),
Martin Luther King (civil rights activist)

Traditions: baseball, basketball, gridiron football

Traditional food: hamburgers, hotdogs

The United States of America is a large country with mountains,
forests and deserts. Most people in the United States of America
live in cities and most of the land is used for farming.

The island of Hawaii is the
only American State not on the
North American mainland.

The Golden Gate Bridge in San Francisco is
a well-known American landmark.

23

Mexico and the Caribbean

There are 14 countries in Mexico and the Caribbean region. Use the key below to find out about and compare each country's languages, religions, ethnic groups, agriculture and natural resources.

Country	Languages	Religions	Ethnic groups	Agriculture	Natural resources
Antigua and Barbuda					
Bahamas					
Barbados					
Cuba					
Dominica					
Dominican Republic					
Grenada					
Haiti					
Jamaica					
Mexico					
Saint Kitts and Nevis					
Saint Lucia					
Saint Vincent and the Grenadines					
Trinidad and Tobago					

Key

Languages	Religions	Ethnic groups	Agriculture	Natural resources
Creole	Christian	African–American	Cereal grains	Bauxite
English	Hindu	American	Citrus	Copper
French	Islam	Asian	Coffee	Gold
Hindi	Traditional beliefs	East Indian	Cotton	Hydropower
Spanish		English	Dairy	Iron ore
Traditional languages		European	Fruit and vegetables	Lead
		Spanish	Sheep, cattle and goats	Nickel
		Mestizo	Sugar	Oil and gas
		Mulatto		Salt
				Silver
				Timber
				Zinc

24

Mexico in focus

Official name: United Mexican States

Area: 1 972 550 square kilometres (761 602 square miles)

Population: 105 million

Capital: Mexico City

Major cities: Acapulco, Tijuana, Guadalajara, Oaxaca, Cancun

Colonial rule: Spain

Famous landmarks: Teotihuacán ruins, Popocatepetl Volcano, Palenque Mayan Ruins

Famous people: Frida Kahlo (artist), Carlos Santana (musician), Pancho Villa (freedom fighter)

Traditions: piñatas (pâper maché container filled with lollies to smash), Mexican sombrero hats

Traditional food: tacos, enchiladas, burritos (beans, beef or chicken wrapped in flat corn and flour breads), guacamole (avocado dip)

Mexico is covered by deserts in the north and by tropical rainforests in the south. It has a rich history including the ancient civilisations of the Olmecs, Aztecs and the Maya. The ruins of these cities are found around the country. Most Mexicans live in cities. Mexico City is one of the biggest cities in the world.

Mexican rugs for sale near Oaxaca. The patterns are based on traditional Native American designs.

Cuba in focus

Official name: Republic of Cuba

Area: 110 860 square kilometres (42 803 square miles)

Population: 11 million

Capital: Havana

Major cities: Santiago de Cuba, Holguin, Pinar del Rio

Colonial rule: Spain

Famous landmarks: El Yunque (flat topped mountain), Capitolio in Havana (parliament building)

Famous people: Fidel Castro (political leader), Desi Arnez (actor), Gloria Estefan (musician)

Traditions: Cuban music and dance

Traditional food: chicken, beans, rice

Cuba is the biggest island in the Caribbean Sea. The land is made up of both mountains and plains where crops are grown.

Cuban musicians and dancers perform for tourists.

Central America

There are 7 countries in Central America. Use the key below to find out about and compare each country's languages, religions, ethnic groups, agriculture and natural resources.

Country	Languages	Religions	Ethnic groups	Agriculture	Natural resources
Belize	■ ■ ■ ■	✟	👤 👤 👤 👤	✿ ♣ ☐	◆ ◆
Costa Rica	■ ■	✟	👤 👤 👤	✱ ♣ ☐ ✤ ☆	◆ ◆
El Salvador	■ ■	✟	👤 👤 👤	✱ ☐ ✤ ◎ ☆ ✿	◆ ◖
Guatemala	■ ■	✟ ✿	👤 👤	☐ ✤ ✤ ✱ ☆	◖ ◆ ◆ ◆
Honduras	■ ■	✟	👤 👤 👤	☐ ✱ ✤ ✿ ☆	◆ ◆ ◆ ◆ ◆ ◆ ◆ ◆ ◆
Nicaragua	■	✟	👤 👤 👤 👤	✱ ♣ ☐ ✿ ◎ ✤ ☆	◆ ◆ ◆ ◆ ◆ ◆
Panama	■ ■	✟	👤 👤 👤	☐ ✤ ✤ ✱ ☆	◆ ◆ ◆ ◆

Key	Languages	Religions	Ethnic groups	Agriculture	Natural resources
	■ English	✟ Christian	👤 African–American	✤ Cereal grains	◆ Copper
	■ Garifuna	✿ Traditional beliefs	👤 Native American	✿ Citrus	◆ Gold
	■ Spanish		👤 Creole	✱ Coffee	◆ Hydropower
	■ Traditional languages		👤 European	◎ Cotton	◆ Iron ore
			👤 Mestizo	✿ Dairy	◆ Lead
				♣ Fruit and vegetables	◆ Nickel
				☆ Sheep, cattle and goats	◖ Oil and gas
				☐ Sugar cane	◆ Silver
					◆ Timber
					◆ Zinc

Guatemala in focus

Official name: Republic of Guatemala

Area: 108890 square kilometres
(42042 square miles)

Population: 13 million

Capital: Guatemala City

Major cities: Puerto Barrios, Huehuetenango,
Puerto San Jose

Colonial rule: Spain

Famous landmarks: Lake Atitlan,
Tikal (Mayan ruin)

Famous people: Rigoberta Menchu
(Nobel Peace Prize winner)

Traditions: Mayan weaving and clothes

Traditional food: beef, chicken, beans, rice

Guatemala is a mountainous and volcanic country. Some of the
volcanoes are still active. Other volcanoes are extinct and lakes have
formed in their craters such as Lake Atitlan. Ancient Mayan ruins are
spread around the country.

At this Christian festival in Guatemala a
statue of a saint is taken from the church
and carried around the village.

Costa Rica in focus

Official name: Republic of Costa Rica

Area: 51100 square kilometres (19730 square miles)

Population: 4 million

Capital: San José

Major cities: Liberia, Puntarenas, Puerto Quepos

Colonial rule: Spain

Famous landmarks: Poas, Arenal and Irazu
volcanoes, Mount Chirripo

Famous people: President Oscar Arias (Nobel Peace
Prize winner and political leader)

Traditions: painted cartwheels, bull fighting

Traditional food: comida (beans, beef or chicken with
rice and vegetables)

The volcanic lake of Poas Volcano
is full of acidic water.

Costa Rica is a mountainous country with large areas of tropical
rainforest. Many animals and plants living in these rainforests are
protected in national parks. Costa Rica has many active volcanoes
such as Arenal, which erupts with smoke and lava nearly every day.

North America's future

There are both rich and poor people living in North America. The biggest goal for North America is to find more jobs, improve health and schooling for the poor people.

Challenges

North America is a continent of huge cities, especially Mexico City, New York and Los Angeles. Toronto, Managua, Guatemala City and San Salvador are also large cities. These big cities use up lots of electricity and energy. Finding enough coal and oil to make power is getting harder. The challenge is to find other more sustainable ways of making energy, such as using the wind and sun.

Some industries produce waste products that can cause air and water pollution. Cities such as Mexico City and Los Angeles also

New York is a very busy city.

suffer pollution from the exhaust of millions of cars and trucks. Air pollution can cause health problems for people. To reduce pollution, smaller cars are being built and industries are being encouraged to decrease waste.

Goals

North America leads the world in technology and industries. Technology is needed to discover new cures for disease, to explore space and to make people's lives easier. The United States of America and Canada lead the way in researching new technologies. Silicon Valley in California is a large centre for computer research. Other countries such as Mexico are leaders in manufacturing. Many North American countries trade freely with each other. More trade creates jobs for the people. When the people in poorer regions such as Central America are working, they can afford better education and health care for their children.

Not all industries in North America are involved in new technologies. These Guatemalan children wear hand-embroidered traditional clothing.

North America in review

North America is the third largest continent.

Area: 25 million square kilometres
(9.3 million square miles)

Population: 480 million people

First humans in North America:
15 000 years ago

First civilisations: Olmecs, Mixtecs,
Zapotecs, the Maya, Aztecs, Native Americans
such as Hohokam and Navaho

Countries: 23

Biggest country: Canada

Smallest country: Grenada

Most crowded country: Barbados

Highest point: Mount McKinley in Alaska,
United States of America, at 6194 metres (20 322 feet)

Longest river: Mississippi River in the United
States of America at 6019 kilometres (3740 miles)

Climate zones: arctic, temperate, arid, tropical

North American regions: Canada and the United States of America
(the North), Mexico and the Caribbean, Central America

Most common languages: English, Spanish, French,
traditional languages

Websites

For more information on North America go to:
http://www.worldatlas.com/webimage/countrys/na.htm
http://www.kidsforcanada.ca/
http://elbalero.gob.mx/kids

Glossary

ancestors   distant relatives from the past

arctic   extremely cold climate at or near the North Pole

arid   a dry, desert-like climate

colonised   when one country takes over another

Commonwealth   an organisation of 53 countries, many of which once belonged to the British Empire

coniferous   trees that have cones for their seeds

deciduous   trees that loose their leaves before winter

economy   planning how a country makes money

ecotourism   visiting a country to see animals, plants and national parks

equator   an imaginary line around the middle of the Earth's surface

ethnic groups   types of people who share similar heritage

extinct   when no more of a particular species of plant or animal are left on the Earth

gold leaf   gold that has been beaten into a very thin sheet

government   a group of people that run a country

humid   when there is a high amount of water vapour in the air

hydropower   power made by fast-flowing water

independent   a country that governs itself

indigenous groups   the original people of a country

Maya   an early civilisation of North America (mainly in Mexico and Guatemala)

migrants   people who move to another country to live

Native Americans   the original people of North America, once referred to as Indians

Northern Hemisphere   the half of the Earth north of the **equator**

slaves   people who are forced to work

tectonic plates   large pieces of the Earth's crust that move slowly, causing earthquakes

temperate   a mild climate with wet weather and cool temperatures

traditions   the ways things have been done for many years

tropical   a hot, humid and wet climate found near the equator

tundra   vast, nearly level, treeless plains of the Arctic Circle region

Index

A

agriculture   20, 24, 26
animals   6, 14–15
  bears   14
  jaguar   15
  merychippus   6
  mice   15
  racoon   14
  roadrunner   15
  snakes   15
Aztecs   7, 18, 25, 30

B

borders   4

C

Canada   8, 9, 11, 12, 13,
    17, 18, 20, 21, 29, 30
Caribbean Islands   8, 16,
    17, 18, 24, 25, 30
Central America   7, 8,
    11, 13, 17, 18,
    26–27, 29, 30
Christianity   17, 20, 24, 26
civilisations   7, 18, 25,
    27, 30
climate   12–13
Costa Rica   26, 27
Cuba   18, 24, 25

D

deserts   8, 9, 10, 13,
    15, 23, 25

E

ethnic groups   9, 16,
    19, 20, 24, 26

F

forests   14, 15

G

Gondwana   5
Grenada   8, 18, 24
Guatemala   7, 8, 11, 17,
    19, 26, 27, 28, 29

H

Hawaii   8, 10, 18, 23

I

independence   18
industry   21, 23, 25, 27, 28
Inuits   16, 20

L

lakes   8, 9, 11, 21, 27
land ownership   19
languages   16, 17, 20, 22,
    24, 26, 30
Laurasia   5

M

Maya   7, 17, 25, 27, 30
Mexico   7, 11, 13, 15,
    16, 17, 18, 19, 22,
    24, 25, 28, 29, 30
mountains   8, 9, 10, 17,
    21, 25, 27, 30

N

national parks   27
Native Americans   9, 16,
    17, 19
natural resources   20, 24,
    25, 26
Navaho   16, 17, 30

P

Pangaea   5
plains   9, 10, 21, 25
plants   14–15
pollution   28

R

rainforest   15, 25, 27
religion   17, 20, 24, 26
rivers   8, 9, 11, 17, 30

S

saguaro cactus   15
slavery   9, 16
swamps   9, 11

U

United States of
    America   8, 9, 10, 11,
    12, 13, 16, 17, 18,
    19, 20, 22–23, 30

V

volcanoes   10, 11, 25, 27

W

wars   18, 19